WHAT IS A PENTECOSTAL?

FRED SMOLCHUCK

Gospel Publishing House
Springfield, Missouri

02-0849

5th Printing 1998

Gospel Publishing House, first printing 1988
Springfield, Missouri 65802-1894

International Standard Book Number 0-88243-849-2

Printed in the United States of America

Table of Contents

Preface

I have been an ordained minister of the Assemblies of God since 1938, serving as evangelist, pastor, missionary, Bible teacher, and secretary-treasurer of the Assemblies of God, Michigan district.

This material originally appeared as a feature in the *Detroit News*. Requests for copies led to the printing of this booklet.

It is the sincere desire of both author and publisher that the truths contained within these pages shall be a blessing to Pentecostal and non-Pentecostal believers. Our purpose is to clearly and concisely present the basic beliefs of Pentecostals. The author does not attempt to deal exhaustively with the various aspects of the subject. There are many excellent books that do this quite adequately. This is simply a brief overview.

May these truths motivate spiritually thirsty people to reach God-ward and to drink deeply of His Spirit. It is the work of the Holy Spirit to give life, strengthen, and satisfy.

—FRED SMOLCHUCK

What Is a Pentecostal?

A Pentecostal is a firm believer in the divinity and Lordship of Jesus Christ. He is an ardent witness of the power of the Holy Spirit in his life.

Pentecostal are often called full gospel people because they fully accept the New Testament teachings of Jesus Christ as true for this age.

What does "Pentecost" mean?

The word *Pentecost* means "50th day," but specifically refers to the annual Jewish feast of firstfruits, or harvest, which took place 50 days after the Passover. It was exactly on the Day of Pentecost that Jesus' disciples received the baptism in the Holy Spirit (Acts 2:1–4). This experience completely transformed these men from fearful followers to courageous crusaders. Pentecostals believe that this same experience, the baptism in the Holy Spirit, is for every believer today.

Do Pentecostals speak in tongues?

Pentecostals speak in tongues. *Glossolalia* (the New Testament Greek word translated "speaking in other tongues," or languages) is looked upon as the biblical, initial sign by which a person may know that he has received the baptism in the Holy Spirit. The signs of a dynamic, victorious life and ministry for the Lord Jesus Christ will also follow.

Pentecostals believe that when God promised to bestow

the gift of the Holy Spirit, it was not meant to be confined only to the early Christian church at Jerusalem during the period of the New Testament, but included all believers since that time (Joel 2:28).

After receiving the gift on the Day of Pentecost, Peter declared, "The promise is for you and your children and for all who are far off—for all whom the Lord our God will call" (Acts 2:39).

What is the purpose of speaking in tongues?

The Acts record of those who received the baptism in the Holy Spirit specifically indicates (and at other times strongly implies) that everyone spoke in other tongues and that tongues was the sign of receiving the gift.

Glossolalia edifies the individual believer. The apostle Paul wrote, "He who speaks in a tongue edifies himself" (1 Corinthians 14:4). Under the inspiration of the Spirit, when a believer speaks with tongues, he receives a spiritual therapy for both soul and mind; the experience is most encouraging to his faith and confidence in God.

Tongues—when accompanied by interpretation—are also for the encouragement of the entire congregation. Tongues and interpretation equal prophetic utterance and are God's way of dynamically impressing both believer and unbeliever with His concern and love for us.

How does one speak in tongues?

Speaking in tongues is the spontaneous and ecstatic result of the inspiration of the Spirit on a person's being. The strange words uttered are not premeditated or learned. A person filled with the Holy Spirit will yield his vocal cords and tongue to the divine impulse within him and on the prompting of the Holy Spirit will speak an unlearned language.

The realization that God inspired and led him or her to ecstatically speak in such a language acts as a catalyst to the person's faith: If God can so possess the mind, emotion, and tongue, He can do anything. Glossolalia is not an end in itself, but is a sign of a new dimension, a divinely dynamic force functioning in one's life. It draws attention to the fact that God will manifest himself in and through believing, yielded lives.

When did Pentecostals organize as a church?

The first truly Pentecostal church was composed of the disciples of Jesus who received the *charismata* (the divine gift) on the day of Pentecost. This Pentecostal experience has recurred with regularity throughout the history of the Christian church. But it wasn't until the turn of the century that the present day Pentecostal movement began to take on an organized form.

In the early 1900s Bible-believing Christians of various denominations, dissatisfied with cold, formal worship, began to pray for revival. They longed for a duplication of God's power displayed in early apostolic days.

Almost simultaneously, from various parts of the United States and the world, people began to report an outpouring of the Holy Spirit upon those who had been praying for revival. Word traveled fast. News of the glossolalia stirred many. However, the speaking in tongues that accompanied the gift of the Spirit was not accepted by the denominations. In many cases it was resisted and rebuffed. Pentecostals tried to remain in the churches where they originally worshiped, but opposition forced them to leave and to open places of worship where they could serve God without hindrance.

Who is the founder of the Pentecostal movement?

A remarkable fact of the Pentecostal revival is that it cannot be attributed to the leadership of any one man. It was the spontaneous result of the work of the Holy Spirit in the lives of people who desired to see God work.

Many small, independent congregations of Pentecostal conviction and experience sprung up all over the land. It soon became apparent that some organizational structure would have to be set up if an efficient and successful propagation of the Pentecostal experience was to occur. An exchange of communication opened the way for several conferences. Fearing a repeat of the formal denominationalism that had once hindered them from worshiping freely in the Spirit, the early founding fathers decided to form a cooperative fellowship.

How large a group are the Pentecostals?

The Pentecostals are organized into several groups, all basically believing the same. In some instances the polity and points of doctrine differ slightly, due to the early influence of the churches from which they came.

Over 59 million Pentecostals worship each week worldwide. Among this number, a recent *Yearbook of American and Canadian Churches* listed 31 Pentecostal groups. Some of the larger bodies are the Assemblies of God, the Church of God (Cleveland, Tenn.), the International Church of the Foursquare Gospel, the Pentecostal Holiness Church of God, the United Pentecostal Church, and Canada's Pentecostal Assemblies.

Do Pentecostals favor the ecumenical movement?

Pentecostals believe in a united body of Jesus Christ. But they do not favor organic and organizational unity at the expense of doctrinal compromise. A world church that would submerge the convictions and principles held dear by Spirit-filled believers is not attractive to Pentecostals.

Full gospel people have no hesitancy in cooperating in civic and humanitarian projects. But they find no affinity with groups who repudiate the divinity of Jesus Christ, who refuse to accept the Bible as the inspired Word of God, or who are ultraliberal in their lifestyles.

Do Pentecostals send missionaries?

The Assemblies of God, the largest of the Pentecostal bodies, has mission stations in 147 countries of the world. It has 987 Bible schools and extension programs on foreign soil. They are staffed by 1,762 missionaries and 148,822 national ministers, serving 25,219,790 members and adherents. The annual budget for this work is more than $113 million (1995).

Are Pentecostals emotional?

Pentecostals are emotional, but not unreasonably so. No one thinks a person is odd for reacting emotionally at a ball game or expressing joy when a lost valuable is found. Pentecostals believe it's perfectly normal to react emotionally when one's sins are forgiven or the realization of eternal salvation dawns.

The Bible says: "The joy of the Lord is your strength" (Nehemiah 8:10). Pentecostals feel their religion in addition to believing it. They believe and experience the verse that says: "The Spirit himself testifies with our spirit that we are God's children" (Romans 8:16). The Bible contains numerous promises of joy for those who trust the Lord.

Joy is reflected in the songs that Pentecostals sing, in their prayers, and in their worship. To a Pentecostal, his union with God is real. He communes with God, he feels God's presence, he knows the difference between his present association with Christ and his former days of unbelief. "The old has gone, the new has come!" (2 Corinthians 5:17). A Pentecostal faith is a living one.

Do Pentecostals believe in miracles?

The Bible declares (1 Corinthians 12:1–11) that among the gifts that the Holy Spirit confers on believers are the gifts of healing, divine faith, and the working of miracles. The recorded testimonies of Pentecostals who have experienced miracles in their lives fill volumes, often reading like a second Book of Acts. Many have been healed of diseases, injuries, and maladies. Blind eyes have been opened, abnormalities corrected.

Pentecostals believe that miracles take place when faith in God's power is exercised. Miracles are for the purpose of drawing people to God. The apostle Peter, after healing a lame man, cried out to the adulating crowd: "Why do you stare at us as if by our own power of godliness we had made this man walk?" (Acts 3:12). He urged them to repent and to look to Jesus Christ.

Are Pentecostals interested in education?

Education is highly regarded and young people are urged to attend schools of higher learning. However, a person's dedication to God is considered more important. Pentecostals believe that spiritual standing comes first and intellectual development second. A combination of both is the desired goal. The Assemblies of God owns and operates nine Bible colleges, two colleges of the arts and sciences, one theological seminary, four Bible institutes, and a nontraditional university in the U.S. Two of the colleges also offer graduate degrees. More than 1,000 Assemblies of God churches sponsor elementary or secondary schools.

What types of people are attracted to Pentecostalism?

At one time it was the opinion of many that Pentecostals were made up of the lower socioeconomic strata of society. It was felt that largely the unschooled dominated the membership.

It is agreed that a great number of the less fortunate of our society were attracted to Pentecost. But this is because they found relief and release from their spiritual burdens through the help of the Holy Spirit. The Pentecostal movement still ministers to all classes of society, as the Church did in apostolic days. It has come a long way since its beginnings. Currently listed as members of Pentecostal churches are businesspeople, educators, scientists, executives, people of means and of intellect—all worshiping and serving God together.

The phenomenal growth of this "third force" in religion is sensational evidence of its maturity, stability, and effectiveness.

The major Pentecostal bodies of the United States have banded themselves into a union, calling it the Pentecostal Charismatic Churches of North America. Every three years, Pentecostals from all over the world gather in a predesignated location for a weeklong convention, the Pentecostal World Conference.

Most Pentecostals are members of the National Association of Evangelicals. However, some bodies prefer to remain independent of any interchurch organization.

How are Pentecostal churches financed?

The Bible is quite clear that the method of supporting the work of the church is the tithe. Members are encouraged to give one tenth of their income for the support of the program. Financial support for ministers, churches, schools, and missions comes from the lay members of the local church. Giving is voluntary and members are advised that their gifts are offered to God.

What are the basic beliefs of the Pentecostals?

The majority of the Pentecostals are of the Arminian branch of the Christian Protestant faith. They believe in the divine inspiration of the Holy Scriptures. The Old and New Testaments are the revelation of God to mankind and the infallible, authoritative rule of faith and conduct.

What about the Trinity?

The majority of Pentecostals accept the trinitarian concept of God. God is one, a compound unity manifested in three Persons, coequal in all attributes, yet each Person distinctive in His divine office work.

Is Jesus Christ divine?

Pentecostals acknowledge the deity of the Lord Jesus Christ and subscribe fully to the doctrine of His virgin birth. As the Son of Man, He was completely and truly man. Yet at the same time He was truly the eternal Son of God. He is called *Immanuel,* "God with us."

What about humanity's status with God?

Pentecostals believe that the first two human beings were created good and upright. However, by voluntary transgression they fell from their righteous state and incurred not only physical but spiritual death—eternal separation from God—on themselves and on future generations (Romans 5:12,19).

It is the firm conviction of Pentecostals that humanity's only hope is found in the sacrifice of Jesus Christ, the Son of God. His life's blood was the price of our redemption.

How is a person saved?

Salvation is received through repentance and faith in the Lord Jesus Christ. This results in a spiritual rebirth that is inwardly evidenced by the direct witness of the Spirit and outwardly shown by a life of righteousness and true holiness.

What sacraments are observed?

Pentecostals do not have sacraments as such, but rather observe two ordinances. Water baptism by immersion is commanded by Jesus Christ of all who repent and believe (Matthew 28:19). In the light of this command, the baptism of infants is not practiced. Instead, they are brought to the assembly and dedicated to God by their parents. A person becomes a candidate for water baptism upon experiencing repentance and faith in Jesus Christ. The act becomes one's testimony of being buried with Christ to the old, sinful ways, and of being resurrected with Christ to a new, sanctified life.

Holy Communion is regularly and reverently observed. It is a token of God's love revealed to mankind through the sacrifice of His Son Jesus Christ. The value of its observance is found in its reminding us of the Savior's love, of our responsibility to that love, and of its potential for a more intimate fellowship with Jesus Christ.

How do Pentecostals look at divorce?

Divorce is generally discouraged among Pentecostal groups. The Assemblies of God "positively disapprove of Christians getting divorces for any cause except fornication and adultery (Matthew 19:9)." And when one has been divorced because of such cause, "we recommend that the question of remarriage be resolved by the believer as he walks in the light of God's Word (1 Corinthians 7:15,27,28)" [*Divorce and Remarriage*, p. 20].

Do Pentecostals believe in heaven and hell?

Without doubt our best concept of heaven falls far short of its reality. The Scriptures assure believers of an abode for the faithful. But existence in heaven will be in an altogether different dimension from what we now know. The Bible encourages the faithful to identify with Abraham, who "was looking forward to the city . . . whose architect and builder is God" (Hebrews 11:10).

Hell is decidedly a place for condemned souls. It is spoken of as being a place of "fire," of "outer darkness," of "torment." It will be the place that will forever separate from God those who refuse Him, who have not availed themselves of the salvation that He offers through His Son Jesus Christ.

Do Pentecostals expect Christ will return to earth bodily?

Pentecostals believe that Christ's coming is more than a return in the form of teachings, influence, or church authority and power. The angels told nearly 500 men who saw Jesus ascend into heaven: "Why do you stand here looking into the sky? This same Jesus, who has been taken from you into heaven, will come back in the same way you have seen him go into heaven" (Acts 1:11). Paul declared, "The Lord himself will come down from heaven" (1 Thessalonians 4:16). The purpose of His coming will be, first, to take His people to himself. Later, He will return to earth to judge the nations and to set up His 1,000-year reign.

Do Pentecostals believe in the end of the world?

Since the making of the atom bomb, the end of the world no longer seems ridiculous. The mushroom cloud that inaugurated the nuclear age has the potential to annihilate not just a few countries—but the entire world.

The apostle Peter wrote: "The day of the Lord will come like a thief. The heavens will disappear with a roar; the elements will be destroyed by fire, and the earth and everything in it will be laid bare. . . . But in keeping with his promise we are looking forward to a new heaven and a new earth, the home of righteousness" (2 Peter 3:10,13).

Pentecostals are convinced that the reason for their growth is found in the fulfillment of the words of the Lord: "Not by might, nor by power, but by my Spirit" (Zechariah 4:6).